Interview Questions

"The One Interview Question"

63 Experts & Their One Go-To Question

Dirk Spencer
Corporate Recruiter

Other books available from Dirk Spencer

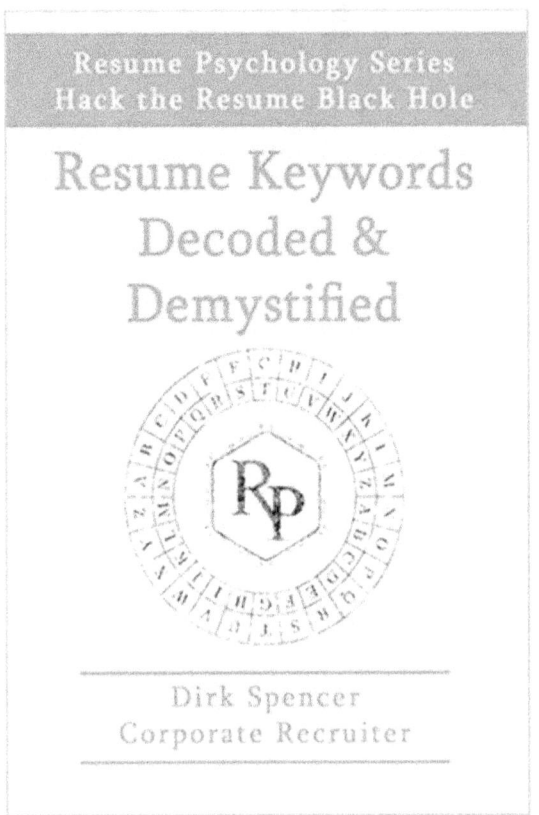

<u>Kindle & Paperback on Amazon.Com</u>
Resume Keywords Decoded & Demystified
Hack the Resume Black Hole

amazon.com

Other books available from Dirk Spencer

Resume Writing Hacks

The Candy Maker Resume

Dirk Spencer
Corporate Recruiter

Kindle & Paperback on Amazon.Com
The Candy Maker Resume
Resume Writing Hacks

amazon.com

Other books available from Dirk Spencer

Kindle & Paperback on Amazon.Com
Resume Psychology
Beat the machine. Be seen. Get hired.

Interview Questions:
"The One Interview Question"
63 Experts & Their One
Go-To Question©

Copyright © 2016 by Dirk Spencer All rights reserved.

No part of this publication may be reproduced, stored in a retrieval system, or transmitted, in any form or by any means, electronic, mechanical, photocopying, recording, or otherwise, without the prior written permission of the author. Printed in the United States of America. For information, contact Dirk Spencer via LinkedIn.

Although the author and publisher have made every effort to ensure that the information in this book was correct at press time, the author and publisher do not assume and hereby disclaim any liability to any party for any loss, damage, or disruption caused by errors or omissions, whether such errors or omissions result from negligence, accident, or any other cause.

No warranties are implied and none can be granted. Information contained herein may not be applicable to your situation. Neither the author nor publisher shall be liable for loss or profit or any damages.

Table of Contents

More People Networking is Required 8

Introduction 9

    63 Was the Number 9

    The Goal: Understanding Interviewer Objectives 10

My Backstory with Interviews 11

My Recruiting Experience 11

What Hiring Managers Want to Know 12

The Top 63 Interviewers 12

What Started My Research 13

    The Candidate's Answer 14

    Recruiters Are Removed from the Outcome 15

    Ask the Hiring Manager 15

Source Data - Finding Examples 16

The Article Excerpts 17

The Interviewer Has a Goal 25

Identifying Interview Goals by Topic 26

Collecting the Data 27

I Hate Math 27

Explaining the Math 28

Here is an Example 29

Calculator Time 29

Fudging the Numbers 30

The Shocking Find 31

What We Hear Versus What They Say 31

My "Gut" Reaction 32

Prepare for Your Interview 33

Career Anthropology 34

Thank You for Reading Along! 36

Dirk Spencer – BIO 37

Dirk's Web Page Information 39

Interview Psychology Online Class & Podcast 39

Dirk's Media Mentions 40

Other Books by Dirk Spencer 42

More People Networking is Required

This is my disclaimer about resumes, social media and interviews: Networking with people *in your profession* is by far the fastest path to your next job! The problem appears to be we woefully *underestimate* how much effort goes into networking with people and how much networking is necessary to find success.

Networking means to *go out* and *interact* among people in your profession. Go be among people in your career space. Stop networking in the wrong places.

Your goal is to be with professionals who do what you do at each networking event, meet-up, or happy hour possible. The more, the better. There is a saying; you can never be too thin or too rich. Same goes for networking, you can never network too often.

The events you attend should have people who could be your future boss or co-worker or they are heavily connected to people who could be your future boss or co-worker.

Where there is a scheduling conflict between professional networking and other activities, go to the networking events first. Being with people and meeting new people in your profession is the surest route to a new job while employed, under-employed or unemployed.

Done effectively, you may land a job without ever taking an interview. That is the power of networking with people in your profession.

Introduction

Interview Questions: "The One Interview Question" 63 Experts & Their One Go-To Question was going to be part of my 4th book *Interview Psychology – Preparation Attracts Offers*. However, it seemed to me not everyone would be interested in this specific piece of research, hence this stand-alone eBook. My goal is to provide a perspective on interviews which might ease your mind on the purpose and reasoning for the questions you experience.

63 Was the Number

We review 63 interview-experts associated with media-articles entitled: "The one interview question" and its variations:

- The One Interview Question I Ask All Candidates
- The Job Interview Question I Ask My Candidates
- The One Job Interview Question I Ask Every Candidate
- The One Interview Question I Ask Every Potential Hire
- One Interview Question You Should Ask Every Candidate
- The One Question You Must Ask Candidates in Every Interview
- The One Interview Question That Will Help You Make the Best Hire

Do not panic when you see the list has 64 entries. It was 63 unique people with one Chatty-Charlie in the group very comfortable describing all of his thoughts.

Otherwise, this was a lot of Google searching. It allowed me to combine natural language search with Boolean search operators to weed out false positives. False positives were articles which used the same words but in a different context and therefore provided no value to our purpose.

The Goal: Understanding Interviewer Objectives

We assess what these interviewers expect to learn from candidates using their "silver-bullet" question.

We also rank each topic or agenda item to establish a hierarchy of expectations based on all the stated objectives.

My Backstory with Interviews

As a recruiter, you are front and center with interview outcomes. My experience with boutique, agency, corporate and contract recruiting gives me a unique overview of different types of interviews as well.

As a recruiter, we see interview styles or types come and go in and out of fashion. Typically, a change in leadership or a new technology facilitates these changes and not always a thought-out or well-reasoned argument. With new leadership, there is pressure to make an impact and showcase your value. With new technology, it seems reasonable to believe a vendor's promise of better outcomes using their products.

My Recruiting Experience

My recruiter and sourcing experience includes staff, management and executive level talent. The job functions I have recruited for include IT for both software development and software architecture, wide area and local area networks, help desk, quality control, accounting, finance, human resources, payroll, corporate communications, training, marketing, social media, and sales to name a few areas.

These job families have given me a front row seat to the rejections, offers, acceptances, counter-offers, and no-show candidates along with hiring biases, bad processes, and bad faith behaviors during the interview cycle.

All of this experience has provided me with some of the most candid feedback on what constituted a failed interview – which led to the original speaker presentations and now book *Interview Psychology* (available on Amazon.Com).

What Hiring Managers Want to Know

What made this research interesting is that it defies about 90% of the conventional wisdom on what hiring managers want to accomplish in an interview.

And while my sample size is not broad enough, the data comes from publish articles and blog responses on 1) What is your go-to question and 2) why is that your go-to question.

Perhaps these results will explain your experiences and or help you prepare more effectively for the next interview.

The Top 63 Interviewers

This research effort is not scientific. It might be more accurate to call this an exploration or examination of interview questions and their purpose.

Regardless of the label, what we review here should provide an insight into the mind of the hiring manager when asking their "the one question." At a minimum we should be able to identify a pattern we can use to be better prepared for interviews.

What Started My Research

While converting the presentation *Interview Psychology – Preparation Attracts Offers* into a book, this random thought popped up: "*What do the top 10, 20, 30; the top 50 interviewers want to know about candidates?*

My context for *Interview Psychology* was rather simple: establish a baseline of behavioral awareness. Too often people come to the interview thinking it is a friendly and honest exchange. This notion puts people in a frame of mind where they are too casual or familial with the interviewer. Or worse, their nervousness gets the better of them which negatively impacts the interview outcome.

Teaching people what the base-behaviors should be and how to prepare is one thing and it deserves its own review.

But - what do the top interviews do? What is their approach to cracking the code on their candidates? Is there a one-size fits all interview question? What is the purpose of this question? What can we learn from such an approach?

The Candidate's Answer

Put another way, what do these hiring managers want to know from of the candidate's answers? Would the answer really be helpful? Would the answer prove or explain the candidate's skills, abilities, and or performance norms?

Instead of guessing or assuming an answer, why not ask these hiring managers?

This approach takes the assertion out or the answer. It also eliminates our bias and opinion and replaces it with their context.

To do this, we can go to the source of the data. We can reach out to the people asking these types of interview questions or we can review their interviews!

Also, I did not want to regurgitate the staffing or outplacement firm suggestions masquerading as free "advice" from vanity press releases designed to sell their brands and services. I wanted to avoid any public relations (PR) in hopes of gleaning true interview insights.

Recruiters Are Removed from the Outcome

Whether in house recruiter or outside staff augmentation, recruiters are one (or more levels) removed from the hiring manager's *needs*.

Recruiters rarely work with the people we find who accept offers and become co-workers at our company.

We rarely interact with the people who land once they start the job either. Unless we bring on HR or other recruiters, recruiters typically do not work alongside new-hires.

If the recruiter is impacted by a new hire, it is *remotely* through a metric designed to measure "hire satisfaction." If this metric is used it should be noted, we do not control or monitor the variables which make-up this metric.

But the hiring manager? She would be directly impacted by a new hire in most cases. Why not go to the source then? Why not ask the hiring managers?

Ask the Hiring Manager

So, why not ask the hiring managers who do the interviews what they expect to discover? Why not ask the top-level professionals, the people sought out by the media? Why not ask what these people want to achieve from *their* interview questions? We can collect their answers and review them for insights!

Source Data - Finding Examples

Recruiters do a lot research on job criteria, functions, career history, skills and the candidate populations in those job families. There is a lot of white-hat hacking, and sometimes direct begging for information to find qualified people to understand a specific profession or set of skills.

In this case, deciding on what to research did not take long. There was an article posted to one of the online portals titled: "*The one question I ask every candidate.*" Wa-lah (the English form of the French "voila") I would use this phrase (and variations) as part of my search string. The result was approximately "63" interviewers who were mentioned in this category. The outcome produced this high-level list of items to track:

- What the interviewers asked
- The reason they asked or the purpose of the question
- The interviewers' complaint about interviewee's answer
- How candidates failed based on their answers

The Article Excerpts

What follows is the redacted excerpts from those articles. I purposely removed the introductions and company or product sales pitches.

I also removed political and sexist commentary. I also saw no value in the interviewers' back story, career rise, industry or other biases listed in the piece.

I wanted the focus to be on the interviewers' questions and expectations. You can skip the excerpts if you like. There are listed here instead of in the back. If you skip this, no one is watching... go...

1. "I'm surprised how many times people talk about the benefit of the job from their point of view, versus the benefit that they're going to bring to the company," This helps him judge whether a candidate is joining a team or whether "it's all about me.

2. "A candidate's hobbies and interests are not fodder for small talk. When one job seeker mentioned that he was a keen singer, "I told him to sing for us, a very senior panel of executives," His assessment: He had the gumption to do it, and he sang very well. To me, it meant he was passionate and able to build skills on his own. And when the crunch time came, he had no hang-ups. We need people with that sort of belief and passion"

3. Besides asking questions that reveal who the candidate was in the past, [it can] help reveal who the candidate has the potential to be in the future, when he/she would be working for your company.

4. Bosses want managers around who won't panic when things go wrong and are self-aware enough to recognize if their own actions might be the source of the problem. Vague answers in which candidates only paint themselves as bystanders to failures foisted upon them by outside forces do not build confidence. [The] challenge [is to get] the respondent to be specific, and […] show maturity and introspection.

5. By the time I interview someone, several people whose opinion I trust have already signed off on them, so I'm really just trying to get to know the candidate. I try to get a sense of why they do what they do, their background, and what motivates them. At the end of the day, it's really important to hire people who contribute to the culture in a positive way. [Can] they pass [the] "airplane test"? That is, "Could I sit on a plane from New York to LA with you and not be bored out of my mind?

6. [The question] catches people a little off guard so answers aren't rehearsed; frequently gives you interesting insight into skills/interests/values they might have that don't otherwise necessarily come to light (teaching swimming vs selling knives door to door versus retail versus food services, etc.).

7. [Question] shows whether a person can think on their feet and it helps drill down into what they are most passionate about. "This forces a candidate to think about what they love doing and what they don't want to do," [the second question] is "a good way to see a person's level of self-awareness.

8. [Focus] on resilience, creativity, and humility in candidates. A person who can speak openly, honestly, and specifically about their personal shortcomings is attractive, but only if they can also explain how they are "a better person, partner, leader, and manager as a result.

9. Great way to hear how people think of risks and rewards.

10. He finds it a great resource to see how they solve problems and also whether or not this is just another job interview or something they are truly passionate about.

11. [Question is to] help job candidates feel comfortable in the interview, "because obviously you get to better see who they really are when they're comfortable. How they respond also allows you to get a deeper sense of them, and if they might be a good fit with your company's culture."

12. I learn whether they've had any sort of relationship with [our company]. If they've never been, have they spent time understanding what we're about? They've either done their homework or they haven't.

13. "I like to watch how they handle themselves in an unstructured environment; "I give them the wine list." The person has to convince the group that they know a lot about wine, or pretend that they do, or just pick the most expensive bottle, or ask for help. How they choose and how successful they are in explaining themselves is one part of the test. Also: "You watch how they treat the waiter," Another test comes at the end: "We always surprise them by asking, 'Tell me a joke.'" This reveals whether someone has a sense of humor, of course, but also whether they can think on their feet in a strange and unfamiliar situation."

14. [Ultimately] it gives insight into who the person really is. "If someone hates making cold calls, but loves data analysis, it's important for you to determine that distinction because each requires totally different skill sets.

15. I try to understand the person's motivations and interest. I also try to understand where they want to take their career and how [company name] fits within that path. Lastly, I'm looking to gauge their intellectual curiosity.

16. I want to determine if the candidate had a strategic understanding of the business. Surprisingly few candidates can answer this question. I am especially impressed by

candidates who have a grasp of existing competitors, potential competitors and what a disruptive, new market entrant could do.

17. If someone enjoys doing a specific job or task, they will probably end up being good at it — or at least passionate about it, Brown adds.; "And I think it's so important to harness people's strengths
18. If they ask me what I mean, the interview is over."
19. I'm curious to see how people deal with ambiguity and whether they can have fun while thinking on their feet; Green says she only wants to hire someone who is "innately driven" — "someone who has that force of spirit that powers them through any obstacle that comes their way.; be prepared to challenge the premise of the question
20. in answering these questions, you can see what motivates the candidate, to what standard he bases all his other actions on, and what kind of person he is.
21. "In truth, there are no wrong answers, but people who practice and read how to give the perfect interview are always flabbergasted.
22. I want to know how they sound when they are passionate about something, and make sure they love the internet. You can teach the rest."
23. insight into a person's character and willingness to continue learning.
24. It speaks to the alignment of goals, resource allocation and priorities and ability to tie different moving parts i.e. people .. that are hard to measure and which make or break the company
25. It tests: the candidate's: ability to prepare; passions; ability to teach; ability to present ideas. It does not: penalize people who are bad at thinking on their feet; have a right answer; bore you if you ask it too often.; t's usually a "fun"

question for the candidate to answer, or if they don't find this kind of question fun, I probably don't want to hire them. (Unlike "what's your biggest weakness?" or "here's this brain teaser I know the answer to but you don't; struggle in front of me") Finally, and importantly, it's un-"game-able" meaning that it does not favor candidates who have practiced interviewing, read threads like this one, etc.

26. It's not 'if' but 'when.' You get surprisingly honest answers when people realize you're going to get a real honest answer from a third party.

27. Millennials are leaving their employers twice as fast as those from older generations, making average tenure in a job about three years. With that said, I look for hiring opportunities that could surpass that time period. We invest in the employee's development to keep them motivated to do great things because it aligns with their long-term career goals-- which is a win for the company.

28. "Most people find their first few jobs on general postings, online listings, job fairs, etc., so that's certainly not a red flag.

29. But candidates who continue to find each successive job from general postings probably haven't figured out what they want to do... and where they would like to do it. Generally speaking those people are just looking for a job; often, any job.

30. And that probably means they aren't particularly eager to work for you. Again, they just want a job and yours will do... until something else comes along.

31. "Plus, by the time you get to job three, four, or five in your career and you haven't been pulled into a job by someone you previously worked for, that's a red flag,"" Younger says. ""That shows you didn't build relationships, develop trust, and display a level of competence that makes someone go out of their way to bring you into their organization.""

32. And that's why being pulled in to a job is like a great reference; people don't hire people they really know unless those people are awesome.

33. "What did you like about the job before you started?""

34. In time, interviewees should describe the reason they took a particular job for reasons more specific than ""great opportunity,"" ""chance to learn about the industry,"" or ""next step in my career.""

35. Great employees don't work hard solely because of lofty titles or huge salaries. They work hard because they appreciate their work environment and enjoy what they do. (Titles and salary are just icing on the personal fulfillment cake.)

36. That means they know the kind of environment they will thrive in, and they know the type of work that motivates and challenges them -- and not only can they describe it, they actively seek it.

37. "Why did you leave?""

38. Sometimes people leave for a better opportunity. Sometimes they leave for more money.

39. Often, though, people leave because an employer was too demanding. Or because they didn't get along with their boss. Or they didn't get along with co-workers.

40. When that is the case, don't be judgmental. Hold on to follow-up questions and stick to the rhythm of the three questions, because that makes it easier for candidates to be more open and candid when discussing subsequent jobs.

41. Do that and many candidates will describe issues with management or disagreements with other employees or with taking responsibility -- issues they otherwise would not have shared.

42. Then, when you've worked your way through every job, follow up on patterns that concern you.

43. ""The three questions are a quick way to get to get to the heart of a candidate's sense of teamwork and responsibility,"" Younger says. ""Some people never take ownership and always see problems as someone else's problem. And some candidates have consistently had problems with their bosses -- which means they'll also surely have issues with you."""

44. no answer is too ambitious, no right answer, but in practice the role they're interviewing for determines which way the CEO leans. In a collaborative environment, it's better to be respected than feared; at a business unit that's struggling, the stick may be more useful than the carrot.

45. Not the candidates, but people who would have encountered the candidates on their way to an interview

46. One trait that's especially important, Crosby said, is intellectual curiosity, which she defines as a strong ability and willingness to learn new things, demonstration of intellectual curiosity

47. Rational

48. See Inside to the Left

49. sense of how passionate/committed the applicant might be about my industry and the position

50. She believes this questions tells you what matters most to people and where their passions lie. Done is better than perfect

51. Tests how self-aware someone is, and whether they are open-minded

52. The answer gives me a feel for the candidate's curiosity and desire to continue learning, technical interests apart from work experience and how they value the knowledge and

53. experiences of the broader technical community in building their skills and network

54. The answer tells me a lot about what they perceive as their own weaknesses, career regrets and shortcomings

55. The number they give is usually irrelevant to the actual interview, but the way they go about explaining their answer reveals a lot about their character; One of the main characteristics we look for in all of our candidates is a strong desire and passion to learn. I tell people that we are not hiring them for where they are now, but where we think they could eventually grow to become. We look for potential, and the best indicator of a person's ability to improve is their passion for learning.

56. The WHY is most important. Research has shown that high achievers have role models and you want to find out what personal attributes the job candidate admires and hopefully tries to live up to

57. Then, I ask for the answer. When I've been on job interviews, I ask if there is something else they are looking for which they have not seen. The question tends to elicit an honest response and invites an opportunity to address other issues. Sometimes you don't get asked the questions that you want to be asked. Find a way to understand the unspoken questions, so that you can infuse your responses with information to make the best impression possible.

58. "This gives me insight in several things: communication (can they explain the project to me in simple terms), teamwork (how were they working with or reaching to others to achieve the goal), motivation (are they enthusiastic about the most exciting project in their life? if not, then they won't be enthusiastic about any other project), expertise (if I am familiar with the domain I can judge whether the challenges they describe were actually difficult)."

59. This question helps understand the size of the team and true processes they used.

There are no wrong answers for this question

60. This reveals how they view themselves and what is important to them. Their answer can be used as a guide for the rest of the conversation, jumping off from various things they say

61. Usually the last answer or two shows what the person really wants out of life and tells me what they care about the most. It helps me understand what motivates them

62. We only hire people with a clear enthusiasm for what we do, because those are the only kinds of employees who will help you innovate and who can grow with your company

63. you can tell a lot — how fast they think on their feet, how much they actually know about our business, how full of it they are? All good things to know. Plus, I want someone to work for me that actually wants to work for me, not just wants a job.

64. You will be surprised at the outcome - no two people answer alike. This question has worked wonders for me to bring out some key incidents, experiences and the overall philosophy. At [company name], we are keen on hiring team players and attitude comes before aptitude and this has helped shape the conversation to make that determination.

The Interviewer Has a Goal

No kidding, right? Think of it this way: "The interviewer has a goal," duh. This is my attempt to quantifying what these interviewers expected to learn, using the content from their questions. Again, not perfect, but we can begin to measure their objectives by breaking down their questions into discrete or specific ideas or topics.

Identifying Interview Goals by Topic

If we review each question we net 28 discreet ideas, topics or agenda items (I am not happy with the label, but it is all I could come up with).

Some interviewers had a solitary focus or idea to uncover. They had a single agenda item or topic in mind. Other interviewers had 2 or more agenda (or topic) items they expected to assemble from their question.

Many of the topic (agenda) items were repeated by multiple interviewers and this is why we do not have 63, 73 or 100 *unique* topic items. Overall the interviewers were in alignment across industries and position (VP, SVP, CEO, COO, CFO). They were consistently seeking the same or similar insights, too. This was surprising. At this level, they all were on the same page.

This total-number of topic-hits (ideas / agenda items... as you can tell I am struggling with how to label this) was summed

(totaled) to provide a gross number of 93 instances of 28 topics sought out by the interviewers.

Collecting the Data

This is what I did, imagine a spreadsheet with 2-columns. The first column has different words listed representing the topic or agenda items found in the interviewer questions. These words are summaries or simplifications of the interviewer's desire to understanding the candidate; specifically, how candidates "think" or their "passion" or their "goals" and so on. The adjacent column, column number 2, has a number in each cell. These numbers represent how many times each topic or agenda item was mentioned by the interviewers. Technically, these numbers are individual subtotals for each word they represent. These subtotals are our "smaller" number. This "smaller" number will be divided by our gross number, what I will call our "bigger" number in a moment.

I Hate Math

We total all the subtotals (our smaller numbers) in the second column to yield the gross-total of how many times all the agenda or topic items were mentioned. This is our gross population of topic items.

In this case, the gross-total was 93; our "bigger" number.

Explaining the Math

This means we had 29 unique topics (agenda items) repeat for a total of 93 times. This means some of the topics were mentioned once. Other topics were mentioned several times. It is this combination of repeat mentions that creates the number 93.

This means, ninety-three (93) is our gross-total, gross-number, our "bigger" number (apologies for the redundancy here).

Then we can take the individual number, the smaller number in each individual cell (the sub-total by each word) next to each topic-word and divide it by the gross-number (93).

The smaller number is divided by the larger number on purpose (small-number/bigger-number). This simple division operation will net a percentage (I hate math).

This percentage represents how the sub-total for each topic ranks as a ratio (percentage might be the better word here) against the total number of topics mentioned of 93. (Please Google "division" or "ratios" if you need a refresher better than my explanation (I am not a math person)).

Here is an Example

For example, "think," was mentioned 16 times. We divide 16 by 93 to net a percentage representation (or a ratio) of how often "think" showed up in the conversations; compared to all other topics which were mentioned.

Put another way, how does the 16 mentions of "think" stack-up or rank against the total topics (given the total of all other topics-mentioned)? (Phew).

Calculator Time

If we take 16 and divide by 93 we net a percentage of 17.20%. This means: 17.20% of the interviewers want their interview question to help them understand how their candidate "thinks." This provides a ratio to compare each topic. The topic or agenda item "think" had the highest percentage of all available topics by a significant margin.

The second highest percentage was "passion" followed by "motivation" and "Learn." Here are the respective percentages:

17.20%	Think	6.45%	Culture
11.83%	Passion	4.30%	Curiosity Intellectual
8.60%	Motivation		
7.53%	Learn	3.23%	Curiosity
5.38%	Team	3.23%	Self-Aware
4.30%	Communication	3.23%	Skills

3.23%	Solve Problems	1.08%	Humility
2.15%	Aptitude	1.08%	Innately Driven
2.15%	Challenges	1.08%	Innovate
2.15%	Grow	1.08%	Network
2.15%	Weaknesses	1.08%	Open-Minded
1.08%	Attitude	1.08%	Processes
1.08%	Attributes	1.08%	Shortcomings
1.08%	Career Regrets	1.08%	Resilience
1.08%	Creativity		

Fudging the Numbers

We might be able to group topics if their context is similar. In this instance, the words *passion* and *motivation* are not about *energy* or *enthusiasm* given the context. They were used to describe how people internalize the job at hand; was the candidate serious about the work, the job or company specifically? Or was the candidate simply seeking *any* job? The context for the word "learn" was related to intellectual curiosity and variations on this theme (more *thinking* related activity). Given how the interviewers used the words *think, passion, motivation* and *learn* (*learning*), we could combine their respective percentages:

- 17.20% Think
- 11.83% Passion
- 8.60% Motivation
- 7.53% Learn

If we total these percentages, we beat 45%! This suggests the primary goal of interviewers from this data set is to uncover how a candidate "*thinks*" (provided we understand the context of the words used by the interviewer).

The Shocking Find

What is interesting is *skills* is mentioned by only 3% of these interviewers. This could mean several things; the resume does a good enough job of qualifying individual skills, skill interviews happened in a different session, companies expect to train new hires in their methodology (process, tools, regulations, software) so specific skills are irrelevant... lots of questions we cannot know the answer.

We might combine learning, with intellectual curiosity instead of "think" to arrive at a different interpretation of what interviewers are seeking from their questions. We can fudge the numbers. We can confuse the context. If we do nothing, we still net an interest insight to what these interviewers hoped to find out.

What We Hear Versus What They Say

What else is interesting is the 1% topics! Words like:
- Attitude
- Attributes

- Career Regrets
- Creativity
- Humility
- Innately Driven
- Innovate
- Network
- Open-Minded
- Processes
- Shortcomings
- Resilience

These are things we hear "they" care about all the time when interviewing. If that is true, why did these topics not garner a larger share of the interviewer's interests? Why do these topics rank as low as they did is hard to know? A larger data set might alter the ratio, but would it be significant?

My "Gut" Reaction

My "gut" reaction is simple: hiring authorities and their companies expect a certain minimum set of adult behaviors and skills from grown-ups in the workforce.

Or these topics or agenda insights are (rightly or wrongly) a hold-over from college recruiting initiatives? It is common for recruitment team *members* to move out of college programs to corporate programs. It makes sense they would bring their college hiring baggage (experience) with them. It seems likely they would drum these ideal of *attitude* into their hiring manager's psyche.

Or it might indicate (my rationalization, no hard data to support this idea) companies (hiring managers) realize new hires change their team dynamics anyway (read The Five Dysfunctions of a Team by Patrick M. Lencioni or any PBMOK© or SRCUM© manual on team building) and their expectations are the new hire will manage the forming/storming stages created by their arrival (or not?). Could be a little bit of both even.

Prepare for Your Interview

Realize interview tactics and methods evolve over time and changes take place routinely as HR laws and strategies change.

These changes may or may not alter interview objectives (or tricks) so do your own research to be safe.

That said, when doing research challenge your confirmation biases and find examples or evidence contrary to your assumptions and develop your own interviewer insights and action plan.

Here are two internet searches you can do to help you research interview questions specific to your situation using your preferred search engine. Type in these search strings without the quotes and press enter for results:

- "interview questions [insert job-title]"
- "interview answers [insert job-title]"

Without the quotes, the searches could be:

- "interview questions project manager"
- "interview answers project manager"
- "interview questions aviation project manager"
- "interview questions project manager retail"

Change "*project manager*" to your job title. Change "*retail*" or "*aviation*" to your area of expertise or industry to customize the search for your needs.

Career Anthropology

To gain insights to the historical references (if your experience goes back that far or the changes have been frequent) read articles with older dates and tracing the transition in interview questions based on current posts.

While the searches appear very similarly, doing them independently will allow you to organize and collect the information much easier. These searches will yield multiple sources. You will decide which source to take seriously and which ones to ignore. You can also search for bloggers who focus on interviews, your industry and or specific job title to round out all your edification.

For published articles, if the interviewer has changed companies there is a good chance they are still willing to talk about the topic. A little initiative can net you a 5-minute call with an expert or published author if you are willing to make a few calls or send a few thought-out emails.

Thank You for Reading Along!

People willing to read your words is gratifying and a gift to any author; I am no different. Thank you so much.

It pleases most authors to know you have taken the time read these words, give them some thought and agree or disagree with the assessment. It's all good.

My goal was to expose interviewer expectations based on external sources. The aim was to help people prepare for their interviews or have more insight to the objectives. With this data and your own research, your interview skills and confidence will improve and allow you to generate more offers.

To your best interview yet,

Dirk Spencer

Recruiter
Creator of Resume Psychology & Author of:
Resume Psychology: Resume Hacks & Traps Revealed, Beat the Machine, Be Seen & Get Hired!
The Candy Maker Resume
Resume Keywords Decoded and Demystified
Interview Psychology – Preparation Attracts Offers
Networking Psychology – Connecting to People on Purpose

Dirk Spencer – BIO

Dirk Spencer is a former government analyst, turned corporate recruiter, public speaker and published author.

Mr. Spencer leverages his former programming and systems analyst expertise to explain the people, processes and technology impacts on the modern resume and what it takes to be great at job interviews.

Dirk has presented at professional associations and career transition groups from Dallas to Denver.

His books are available on Amazon.Com.

As a LinkedIn open networker Dirk accepts all connection requests. Invite him to connect with you and gain access to his first-degree connections.

His web sites include DirkSpencer.Com and ResumePsychologytheBook.Com with a blog on Google and additional content on multiple platforms.

While networking with professionals in your area of expertise is by far the most empowering method to being re-hired; they will eventually schedule an interview. Come over-prepared!

Mr. Spencer has presented Resume Psychology, The Candy

Maker Resume and Resume Keywords Decoded and Demystified and Interview Psychology to professional associations including: Pikes Peak Recruiter Network, Inter-City Personnel Associates, Executive Search Owners Association, American Society for Quality Conferences, National Investor Relations Institute, International Institute of Business Analysis, Intuit Women's Network, Texas Workforce Commission and Dallas Fort Worth Texas Recruiters Network (DFWTRN).

He has also volunteered his time to present these concepts to Career Transition Groups such as: Career Jump Start FUMC Richardson, Carrollton Career Focus Group, Carrollton City Job Hunt 101, Crossroads Bible Church Career Transition, Fort Worth Career Search Network, FWCSN Resume Boot Camp Job Angels Network, MacArthur Blvd Baptist Church, Preston Trail Job Network, McKinney Workforce Networking, Southlake Focus Group.

Dirk has also presented to diverse ecumenical groups including: Jewish Family Service (JFS), Career Counseling Group of DFW Islamic Association of North Texas (IANT), Career Counseling Group of DFW Islamic Center of Irving (ICI),

McKinney Trinity Presbyterian Church Career Transition Network, St. Philip's Episcopal of Frisco Job Ministry, St. Andrew UMC Sales Group, St. Jude Career Alliance a Chapter of the Catholic Career Development Community.

In his off-time the Dirk does amateur nature photography, makes Christmas decorations year-round and folds origami-crafts.

Dirk's Web Page Information

http://resumekeywordsdecoded.teachable.com/
- Resume Keyword Online Class -

http://www.dirkspencer.com/
- Focused on my recruiting expertise

http://www.resumepsychologythebook.com/
- Focused on the book versus the lecture series

http://resumepsychology.blogspot.com/
- Focused on recurring resume questions

Interview Psychology Online Class & Podcast

The online class is on Teachable.Com. This is 30 minutes of video divided into 2 to 3 minute segments. Learn how to find & select resume keywords for your specific area of expertise. Master the "what to do" and "how to do it" for your resume keyword needs. As of this publication date – the class is Free.
http://resumekeywordsdecoded.teachable.com/

Dirk's Media Mentions

Resume Keywords Decoded Feature Article
https://www.recruiter.com/i/stop-calling-yourself-an-entrepreneur-and-other-resume-keyword-tips-from-a-resume-psychologist/

Named to the Top 25 Resume Building Career Blogs
http://www.personalincome.org/top-25-resume-building-career-blogs/

His book made a 10 Must Buy List... so this was a cool thing to happen in 5 months...
https://www.recruiter.com/i/10-must-buy-books-for-job-seekers

Agency versus Corporate Recruiting Advice with Recruiter Q&A of Recruiter.Com
https://www.recruiter.com/i/recruiting-career-advice-agency-or-corporate/

Four ways out of a recruiting rut with Erin Engstrom RecruiterBox.Com
http://recruiterbox.com/blog/4-ways-to-climb-out-of-a-recruiting-rut/

Beat the Bot – Podcast Interview with Albert Lin of Careers.Org
http://www.careers.org/blog/ep2-beat-the-bots-in-your-job-search-dirk-spencer-does-it-every-day/

Examples of great customer service
http://www.nanorep.com/49-customer-experience-professionals

Eight ways for keeping in touch with candidates Recruiter Q&A of Recruiter.Com
https://www.recruiter.com/i/8-ways-to-stay-in-touch-with-rejected-candidates/

Should You Re-Apply to the Same Job with Elisabeth Greenbaum Kasson of DICE
http://insights.dice.com/2016/01/11/should-you-apply-for-the-same-job-twice/

You May Be an Outdated Job Seeker If... on CareerCloud.Com with Chris Russell
http://www.careercloud.com/news/2016/1/23/the-outdated-job-seeker-part-2

Unlikely Places to Find Work with Recruiter Q&A of Recruiter.Com
https://www.recruiter.com/i/6-unlikely-places-to-find-a-job/

Be a Better Recruiter with Recruiter Q&A of Recruiter.Com
https://www.recruiter.com/i/be-a-better-recruiter-10-simple-tips/

Curve Ball Interview Questions with Matthew Kosinski, Editor at Recruiter.Com
https://www.recruiter.com/i/interview-questions-the-top-10-curveball-questions-and-why-you-should-pose-them-to-candidates/

Other Books by Dirk Spencer

Kindle & Paperback on Amazon.Com
Resume Keywords Decoded & Demystified
Hack the Resume Black Hole
https://www.amazon.com/dp/0692771840

Kindle & Paperback on Amazon.Com
The Candy Maker Resume
Resume Writing Hacks
http://www.amazon.com/dp/0692652698/

Resume Hacks & Traps Revealed
Beat the Machine. Be Seen. Get Hired!

Resume Psychology

Dirk Spencer
Corporate Recruiter

Kindle & Paperback on Amazon.Com
Resume Psychology
Beat the machine. Be seen. Get hired.
http://www.Amazon.Com/dp/0692525602/

www.ingramcontent.com/pod-product-compliance
Lightning Source LLC
Chambersburg PA
CBHW061450180526
45170CB00004B/1640